A LEGACY OF WORDS
A Collection of Poems

Michael Alty

Food for Thought

"It is worth a thought to write your thoughts on paper
As this could be of benefit to you later
Forget the Hash and the common Back Slash
A computer has been known to crash
Unless you are extremely clever
It is possible you may have lost them forever"

Published 2021 by arima publishing

www.arimapublishing.com

ISBN 978 1 84549 781 1

© Michael Alty 2021

All rights reserved

This book is copyright. Subject to statutory exception and to provisions of relevant collective licensing agreements, no part of this publication may be reproduced, stored in a retrieval system, or transmitted in any form or by any means, without the prior written permission of the author.

Typeset in Garamond

This book is sold subject to the conditions that it shall not, by way of trade or otherwise, be lent, re-sold, hired out, or otherwise circulated without the publisher's prior consent in any form of binding or cover other than that which it is published and without a similar condition including this condition being imposed on the subsequent purchaser.

In this work of fiction, the characters, places and events are either the product of the author's imagination or they are used entirely fictitiously. The moral rights of the author have been asserted. Any resemblance to actual persons, living or dead, is purely coincidental.

Swirl is an imprint of arima publishing.

arima publishing
ASK House, Northgate Avenue
Bury St Edmunds, Suffolk IP32 6BB
t: (+44) 01284 700321

www.arimapublishing.com

A City of a Thousand Baguettes

Everyone here seems to be having a feast
Filling their mouths full of carbohydrates and yeast
Munching their way around ten thousand clocks
It's no wonder why they are built like an ox
In Supermarkets there is a danger
That they may bump into a disparaging stranger
As produce start falling off from the shelves
One has to be aware of the unexpected pram
From behind a medieval battering ram
They weave their way round with shopping trolleys
With a point of a finger it's up with their brollies
Still eating away in busy street
A *pain au Chocolat* is a real treat
In a Boutique stands a fine looking dress
As someone with sticky fingers makes it a fine looking
Mess

Then a friend appears looking rather chic
Slaps a dollop of cream upon your lap
Not once but twice if that's not enough
Your face is then covered with a whole load of stuff
After smoothing down her expensive lingerie
Then it's back to the *Boulangerie*
Bent over the counter oooh la la...
She fancies another *pain au Chocolat*
Where is this place you will never know?
I'm looking at it all through a glass of *Bordeaux*

Flowers of Anxiety

Bring not the bluebells
Growing wild on yonder fells
Bring not the 'Gilded Lily'
Abound in distant valley
Bring not the poses and the roses
The sweetness of the pea
But, bring me your love and that is all
To all creatures great and small
Long after winter when snowdrops fall

Blindness

Show me the morning
Show me the night
Show me the stars that twinkle o' so bright
Show me the happiness when sadness made to call
Show me the sunrise when darkness began to fall
Show me the garden that was full of roses
Show me the daffodils, tulip and posies
Show me the ice and show me the snow
Show me the fire and its rich golden glow
Show me the castle which was built in the sand
Show me the reason why this came to be
No one's as blind as those who cannot see

Benghazi Nights

A blue starry sky, it was nearly jade
We chose a table in the shade
The fans did their turn inside the NAAFI
A few years away from Colonel Kaddafi
A world far away from normal life
For some it was separation
                    from the 'Trouble and Strife'
We sat around and nobody cared
The loudspeaker called
It was now time for prayers
With plenty of plenty and lots of good cheer
In a Colonial atmosphere
On the veranda we all played poker
There was always an occasional joker
Who made us laugh with his hand
When a card fell on to the desert sand
Then at midnight on the clock
We all staggered back to the barrack block

This poem is dedicated to those who served with the Royal Army Veterinary Corps, and The Royal Military Police Dog Section, Diosta Barracks and Wavel Barracks, Benghazi, Libya in 1967.

Which is Witch?

To which of these witches are witches with which
You compare all the which-ways
And decide which is which
You choose which one
Whichever you glean
You'll find all the answers in a "Witch Magazine"

Halloween

If you are not into Trick or Treats
Then arm yourself with lots of sweets
They come around with plenty of sacks
Giving people heart attacks
They knock on your door then ring the bell
They try to make your life a bloody hell
They get you into one hell of a state
When they take away your garden gate
They go around looking for things to steal
Then you find that you are minus a wheel
On your car windscreen there is a gooey mess
Just to add to the misery and stress
Next year we are going out on Halloween
And pretend that they have never been

Aliens

A Martian came to watch some cricket
After the match he received a ticket
He said, "I'm not really into cars"
And then flew off back to Mars

'Aussie' Bingo

"At a watering hole in Wanadingo
Tourists sit around and all play bingo
They eat roast Iguana and Red Kangaroo
While listening to a didgeridoo
And, who was it making a noise in the bush?
Some say it was 'Rolf Harris' with his painting brush
And by a lake in front of Ayers Rock
People are eaten by a hungry Crock
Next day it's off to Alice Springs
Where they can shop and buy a few things
An Aborigine says it's such a drag
To come all this way for some chips in a bag
It was back to the hole in Wanadingo
Where they drink from tinnies and all play bingo"

WRVS*

If you're down in the dumps and feeling the blues
There is always the lady with the hat and court shoes
With lots to do whatever you choose
A quick game of 'Poker' you have nothing to lose
And if you fancy a dabble
She comes up with the 'Scrabble'
And if you are tiddly after some drinks
Then it's on to the sofa for a quick forty winks
She talks in strange foreign languages
It sounds like tea and cucumber sandwiches
She smiles all the time there's no-one finer
Sporting a scarf drives a green Morris Minor
She's into Allsorts
The round ones are best
Those hundreds and thousands don't arf stick in your chest
She wears lots of make-up and cares not a damn
If you're familiar and call her a ma'am
If she has helped you then she has succeeded
Her services worldwide are forever needed

*Women's Royal Voluntary Service

Primroses

"In Whitehall they sell primroses,
And in Trafalgar Square
People stop to close set trays
And then carry everywhere
Gold of sprig in poses shining
Through the town's grey morning air
But all those neatly tied bunches by the dozen lying
    there
And all the people in Whitehall and in Trafalgar
    Square
I'd give for this far better thing and give without a
    care
One early primrose bright against this dark wave of
    your hair"

The Royal British Legion
(The Last Bastion of an Empire)

From dark ages past one sees the Light
To defend our country against foreign might
To those past and present we cannot forget
And will be forever in their debt
It is important that we must pray
To keep our sacred "Remembrance Day"

"Victory V's"

There's a Gal that gets up with the Larks
In tracksuit and trainers is seen jogging in the parks
Of grand appearance, she's looking fine
Doing a few laps around the 'Serpentine'
After a swig of 'Sport Lucozade'
She takes the salute from the 'Household Brigade'
A Japanese sniper taking a shot at the ducks
He is hoping to make quite a few bucks
Up with two fingers or maybe the one
She swallows a "Victory V"* and is glad he has gone
Back to his country with something in mind
That thousands of people here have an axe to grind
She sprints to her House in time for the cards
Specially delivered by the 'Grenadier Guards'

---

*A disgustingly sweet aniseed lozenge, which can only be described as a bitter pill to swallow.

Miss Lonely Heart

When the ugly face of Sadness
Turned into madness
When one couldn't speak and others couldn't spout
And unlike the tide, you always came in
But never came out
You ran away for some kind of reason
As I walked through the gardens
In the last 'Summer Season'
Afraid of the chase because of straight lace
You pretended to be true and found someone new
And, in the grounds of the Palace
You met King George, Queen Mary and Princess Alice
They didn't know you were so cold and also callous?
I wondered about you from the very start
You were just another "Miss Lonely Heart"

Communications

When you've had enough of your tutor
And feel you can't hack your computer
Just go back to the old pen and ink
And just relax and start to think
Of nothing better than to send someone
                              a simple letter
And if you do not feel like writing home
Just pick up the 'Dog and Bone'

Symphony in Suet

A pastry construction made with some flour
Carefully rounded and built like the 'Tower'
Inside this sculpture lay mouth-watering savoury
Braised Steak and Kidney in a rich tasting Gravy
Landladies serve them with big mushy peas
They go down well especially at teas
You can buy them at Safeway
But they're not quite the same
Your local chip shop they are to blame

MICHAEL ALTY

A Poem for Bedtime
(Or a Bedtime Poem)

A candle flickers every night
In a room devoid of any light
When you look it's an eerie feeling
As shadows dart from walls to ceiling
Through the window there's one light on
The master has long since been dead and gone
The house that stands on the edge of the wood
You don't go there it's for your own good
You can go if you dare
People say there's no-one there

The Bell Ringer

Every week he thinks it is cool
To ring our door-bell on his way
                home from school
He does a Jennifer Rush by our house
Quicker than any dormouse
Lately he has changed his tack
To ring the bell on his way back
You cannot catch him he is so fast
Like a Tornado he flies past
Under the window with a pack on his back
He thinks its good crack
We have lost track how many times he has
                rung our bell
He is making our lives hell
He is becoming a bit of a bore
I only wish he would knock on the door

'The Grand Old Duke of York'

The Grand Old Duke of York
He had ten thousand quid
He put it into stocks and shares
And then he said his prayers
When they were up they were up
When they were down they were down
And when they were only half-way up
He sent for Gordon Brown

'William Tell'

The Swiss thought it was a hoot
When William was to shoot himself in the foot
At the village fair he had shot his bolt
You can take this with a pinch of salt
He missed the target and hit his friend
But there was a sucker on the end
The man with the prizes looked all forlorn
When William won a '*Toblarone*'

The Next Train to Waterloo

'Good weekend Tom
You are looking brown'
'Yes! Took the kids out riding
The Volvo has broken down
Lucinda has got a new horse
I bought it for her birthday of course
Went to the Club and played a
                few rounds
With this guy called Grant from
          "Horse and Hounds"
Can't wait for the weekend to come
Picking up a new car and that will be fun'

'And what did you do over the weekend Ted?
'I spent most of it in bed
On Friday night I caught a strain
I do believe it was on this train
Well I really must read a few lines
From yesterday's 'Sunday Times'
On the front page they mention the flu
It all started at Waterloo'

Pussycat

"Pussycat, Pussycat where have you been?
'I have been to London to see the Queen'
'And who else did you see when you were there?
'I saw Tony Blair underneath a chair'
'And what did you do when you arrived back?
'I had a word with Jacques Chirac'
'He said like me did you have to bow?
I said no, 'Just mieou.....'"

Wembley Stadium

It was for some the Palladium
When a band stepped out in Wembley Stadium
They marched up and down to a loud hooray
As they played a tune to Freddie Mercury
There was to be a slight hitch
When a drum decided to roll down the pitch
It went down the centre and into the goal
The crowds all went crazy, the show they stole
They carried on playing and doing their drill
The football match ended the score was One-Nil

Trinidad comes to Burnley

'Hey man what's that noise coming down our street?
Why, it's the 'Phonies with the Boney's'
The 'Phonies' with the boney's?
Yea man, it's the 'Phonies' with the Boney's'
And the Loony's with their Tuney's
And once more, who is that banging on our door?
Why it's the 'Bums with the drums'
The 'Bums with the drums'
Yea man, it's the 'Bums with the drums'
They sound like "The Loony Tunes"
After a bad night in "Wetherspoon's"
There is this guy with the biggest knife you ever did see
Why that will be Colin, your regular local, "Crocodile Dundee"
And tonight he will change from his scouting attire
For a Cassock and Surplus, he's in the church choir
And then there's a guy blowing into a pipe
He looks like your brother; you know, the Rastafarian type
And then there's a guy humming a kazoo
I don't suppose he's got nothing else better to do
Hey man, on a Sunday I deserve some *kinda* peace,
                        and, some *kinda* quiet
And not listening to a dude who's in charge of a riot
Can you please close the window, heaven forbid?
Before I start my banging on top of a tin lid
Have they nothing else better to do, than to march on a Sunday
When I was trying to sleep, and praying it was Monday'

The Whistler

We are being driven round the bend
With a neighbour we all call our friend
He is deaf and hard of hearing
To us it is very endearing
His whistling becomes more acute
It is beginning to sound like a Peruvian flute
He whistles away throughout the day
It gets much louder one could say
We are now at our wits' end
He is still driving us round the bend
We are now at the end of our tether
Trying to put a petition together
Ten feet high or even more
He has become the eternal bore
He's still whistling and won't go away
His whistling going on for ever come what may

"Titanic"

"No one can hear the voices from a silent grave
But just a ripple from an incoming wave
Where 'Rogues' lurk and echoes sound
In a silent grave two and a half miles down"

Alfred and his Cakes

Alfred whilst eating his Kellogg's Cornflakes
Decided to bake a few cakes
With some syrup and sugar, nutmeg and flour
He set the timer to read half-an-hour
The alarm went off without any hassle
The cakes came out burnt to a 'frazzle'

Birds in Flight

Uncle Ben thought it very nice
To lay on a bowl of savoury rice
A hen that took to nocturnal flight
When it saw a jar of "Chicken-Tonight"

The Man with the Golden Balls

He sits inside his shop
It is an Aladdin's Cave
Full of artefacts and beautiful things
Most of which he wants to save
He puts beauty inside his money box
And can't afford the door
That hides away the jewellery he dearly
                         wants to store
When he goes out from his well-padlocked flat
You'll find the key underneath the well-untrodden mat
He keeps a close watch on Stock Market falls
He is the man with the Golden Balls!

The Butcher at Christmas

A string of Puddings hang from a hook
And look in the window next to the duck
A pheasant, a goose and a turkey
All to make your Christmas quirky
A tray of pies made today
Dressed with parsley on display
Ready for your party on Christmas day
And in the New Year it's another year on
Outside the butchers in Todmorden

A Wee in the Dee

A wee Scottish Lassie had a wee tartan tie
And a wee tartan haggis hangin fae the thigh
A wee highland safety pin protruded through her nose
A wee Scottish Lassie we oot any clothes
On a Saturday night after a wee beer
She weed a wee wee on the banks of the weir
Up came a wee bobby on a wee mountain bike
And said tae the wee Lassie will ye go for a hike
We you! Said the wee Lassie this must be a joke
I would sooner ma wee haggis or sniff some maer Coke
To the station they went we nae maer ado
and told the wee Lassie its awa tae the loo
It took a wee while tae get oor the wee shock
and tae nae maer go oot wee oot any frock
Now the wee Scottish Lassie wears a wee chequered scarf
a wee chequered hat, tis good for a laugh
Nae maer the wee safety pin in her wee nose
Of that poor wee Lassie we oot any clothes

A Poem for Breakfast Time

When you lose your "Snap, Crackle and Pop"
And conversation comes to full-stop
Through the letter box comes another bill
As the toast burns underneath the grill
When everything costs an 'arm and a leg'
And the wife puts an end to your bacon and egg
Into the bin you feel there is no hope
It is only another envelope
And when it goes to the bottom of the pile
Just sit back and give her a smile

'Everything is important
                      but nothing is that important'

Scooters

In Parka coats designed for the Arctic
We all thought we looked fantastic
Sat astride our 'Vespa' Scooters
Giving it plenty on plenty of hooters
Riding into some strange coastal towns
People said we looked like clowns
Into 'Bars' we would take a break
Good conversation over a milk shake
Putting world to rights around a round table
Trying to avoid the occasional 'Hells Angel'
If I were to have my time back so far
I would not have swapped it for an old 'jam jar'
On looking back it was such good crack
I wish I had my scooter back

Pay Up and Shut Up

For some drivers it is a disgrace
to take an Invalid's car parking space
It doesn't make sense
to tempt providence
Spare a thought for the needy
and stop being so greedy
If you can afford to buy an Espace Six-Seater
then you can afford to put money in a parking meter
If you can't afford to pay
then your car should be clamped and towed away
You take my place
You take my disability
'Pay up and Shut up'

To Hell and Back

"Travelling back down life's highway
This was for me my judgement day
At the end of the road I rang the bell
Before I entered into hell
Keep your hands in your pockets
Said the Grim Reaper
Bellowing out from a loudspeaker
Wait in the room on the ground level
Until it is your turn to shout at the devil
He will decide whether you go or you stay
Before travelling back down life's "highway"

Our Cat

Luda is a Russian cat
She likes to know about this and that
Putin it here and Putin it there
She puts her foot in it everywhere
She marches up and down the house
to find yet another disparaging mouse
She goes underneath the bed
in case she finds a Red
Carpet on the floor
then she makes a bolt for the door
At mealtimes she eats caviar
this comes out from a 'Safeway' jar
She runs around in full throttle
Drinks Smirnoff Vodka straight from the bottle
Luda is our special cat
A typical Russian aristocrat

Davy Crocket

King of the Northwest Frontier
We sat in an Orange Box paddling our canoe
Davy Crocket in the Front Seat
Humming his Gazzooooooo!
In the Back Yard two men in a Boat
Decided one day to cut up a fur Coat
With mum out the Shops and coming home soon
We changed whole specie from Mink to Racoon
The Cat with Nine Lives on the wall did a runner
As water from a Pistol were to give it a stunner
Mum came back from the Shops and found us all out
She gave us a clout and a clip around the Ear
We were the Kings of 'The Wild Marton Mere'

Big Night Out

"Wat dust da want ta drink Bert?
I'd like a Bitter Shandy Bob
A Bitter Shandy Bert
Yeas, a Bitter Shandy Bob
And art havin a drink asweel Bob?
Yeas, a Lemonade Shandy Bert
A Lemonade Shandy Bob?
Yeas, a Lemonade Shandy Bert
Would that be a pint or an arf Bert?
I think I'll just av arf Bob
And art havin an arf asweel Bob?
Yeas, a think it only wise Bert
Would ta like a packet of Crisps Bob?
Yeas, I'd luv a bag of Crisps Bob
Wat flavour a crisps would ta like Bert?
Wat flavours av thi getten behint bar Bob?
I'll ask Barman wat e's getten Bert
And dust ta want any Crisps Bob?
Yeas, am havin a bag of Plain Bert
Blumin eck! Look at blumin time Bob
It's five ta blumin Six Bert
Look at blumin queue at back on us Bert
Bowlers need a blumin seat
It's time we both went huam Bob
It's "Coronation Street" ta neet"

After Shock

A red painted liquid
A Genie in a bottle
Rub the red neck
It's out in full throttle
After the shock there's no
                turning back
The Genie won't go back
Into that red ruddy bottle

Introducing Mr and Mrs Strange

Albert and Gertrude live down our street
This is a couple I would like you to meet
They see more of life than the average family
And when you read more you will agree
That these two characters are 'out of their tree'
Whatever they do and wherever they go
People use windows instead of a door
And there's more.....

They go on holiday three times a year
The airlines say Oh No! And tremble in fear
Some say, "Not these two again"
Why can't they travel by a 'Virgin Train?'
They create mayhem I cannot begin
To tell you what lies within!

Mr and Mrs Strange go to Town

Albert and Gertrude boarded a bus
And caused one 'eck of a fuss
The driver said keep your hands off the bell
They are known in the town as the shoppers from hell
The bus now empty the passengers all fled
Most of them ready to go back to bed
The bell continued to ring the driver said Go!
Away I've had enough its back to the Bust Depot
They went into a store to buy a few things
It was on their way out the alarm bell rings
A detective appeared and searched through their bags
It was something to do with the security tags
They were arrested and put into cells
Far away from any alarm bells
It was a mistake to accuse these two
Of stealing a tube of 'Superglue'
They were released without charge
When Gertrude said I'm going to Sue
Sue is the 'Brief' who sorts out their trouble
When they try to reduce the town to rubble
They went back home on the bus
The driver with a nervous cough
Said why are all my passengers getting off?
Albert and Gertrude at the end
Tried to get up on to their feet but found they were
                                       both stuck to the seat
The sticky evidence was evident at the last stop
The driver was at the end of his tether
They both fell off the bus together

Action Man

The man that falls on to two deaf ears
Has been around for several years
He goes overboard into the bath
And gets kicked around on the garden path
Then sometimes he is found
Lying on his back on the ground
With a smile on his face looking ever so cute
In his wet and muddy 'Combat Suit'
At night you can find him there
On the bed next to a Teddy Bear

Balls to Niagara Falls

"Underneath a waterfall dry as dry can be
I lost my umbrella when it floated out to sea
Far in the distance and in *ta* dark sunset
A cloud cam *oot fay* the horizon
And then I got bloody wet"

Cecilia Crépe
(As not seen on television)

"Now wash your hands before we start
To make the perfect Bakewell Tart
And don't forget to turn on the oven
And put on a nice clean apron
The one I am wearing has had it's day
The lace around the edges is beginning to fray
On the front it says 'Cook of the Year'
But you can't see this, it's not very clear
Now wash your hands before we begin
These are called Baked Beans in a tin
And now I would like to show you these
They are called Tins of Peas
A perfect standby for all you busy housewives
Watching TV and leading busy lives
And now wash your hands before we try
To make the perfect Apple Pie
Here's one I baked earlier it's very hot
Sorry about the apples I forgot
In the books keep on looking
For Cecilia Crêpe's 'Keep on Cooking' "

Inspector Coppini

The Maltese detective with the whistle and flute
The ladies all think he is very cute
When he swims around in a Polo Match
They all know he's an excellent catch
His side-kick is called Zara
She is a Sergeant from Birkirkara
Zara Borg plays tennis in Mdina
And is often seen in the Yacht Marina
Messing around in boats taking lots and lots of notes
On Sundays Zara is in heaven
When Charlie takes her out in his Mazda RX 7
Charlie Coppini, the man with good looks
He will find himself penned in several books

Cecilia Crépe goes Bombay

"First of all do you see the Sari?
You know I look like Mata Hari
And now I am going to make a curry
So I hope you are not in any hurry
To dash out today to your favourite Indian take-away
Now wash your hands before we commence
You know it makes a lot of sense
The curries I make are very hot
Sorry about the onions I forgot
The sauce I have prepared comes out of a jar
You can get this from your local Spar
One can make this dish in a trice
With lots and lots of *Pilou* rice
And if you want to know where I am coming from
This is called a *Poppadom*
They start off round and kinda flat
I like those and so does the cat
You will find this recipe somewhere in my book
So it's goodbye from Cecilia
And lots of good luck"

Harry the Window Cleaner

Harry continued to be a dreamer
When he decided to become a Window Cleaner
He went to 'Woolworths' to buy his gear
And together with a ladder, his greatest fear
Harry cleaned his windows crystal clear
He knocked on doors to enhance his round
Before climbing high above the ground
Harry was at the end of his tether
When he slipped and fell on his Chamois leather
At a dizzy height things became madder
When he missed a step and fell from his ladder
Into a greenhouse with lots of pots
He found himself lying next to some 'Forget-me-nots'
This was to be another excuse
To become a void
In joining the ranks of Britain's unemployed

Mabel Hibelthwaite

Mabel stands on the doorstep with a brush and a bucket
She chats away to Mrs Vera L. Ducket
They talk about everything and everyone
It makes you wonder just what they are on?

Vera has a hairdresser's shop
She hears all the gossip from Mrs Mop
Who lives down the street a few doors away
And frequents the 'Fish and Chip' shop three times a day
She reads the news from off the grease paper
Then she savours the best bits for later

Mabel sits on a chair for her weekly 'hair-do'
And leaves the 'Salon' a 'Dolly Blue'
She goes to Bingo, there's always a riot
When the numbers are called she cannot keep quiet

Vera's son is considered quite posh
He goes to school in a Macintosh
He thinks he is smart a real ding-a-linger
Drinks his tea with his little finger

Mabel knows when somebody bakes
She has a flair for Eccles Cakes
Mabel is known to be ever so catty
When neighbours call her a "Nora Batty"

Malcolm Ducket

Malcolm the 'Whiz Kid' the sill young fool
Invented a rocket to blow up his school
He went to the Co-op and bought loads of stuff
And mixed it together to call teachers bluff
Back to the Lab with this *Dynamite*
It was all ready to be set alight
The rocket blasted off he said, here is the proof
He's now working part time repairing the roof

Keep on Cooking with Cecilia Crêpe

"If you want a change from bread and jam
Processed cheese and Parma ham
At breakfast time one could go mental
With this stuff they call continental
And if you have a few minutes to spare
I will show you how to prepare
Synchronized breakfast with bacon
and egg sausage and tomato,
mushrooms fried bread and potato
You can even have baked beans to go
This will only take an hour or so
Now wash your hands before you start
I have got this off to a fine art
Now I would like to show you how to make
The perfect Scottish Pancake
Serve them with syrup or marmalade
Here are some I have already made
They look brown straight out from the pan
and they taste delicious with butter and jam
Until next time please buy my tape
Its bye for now from Cecilia Crêpe"

Italian Cuisine

Joey Panzini is the Italian cook
Who doesn't exactly go by the book?
He boils the spaghetti with a sense of fun
When it slides down the walls he knows that it's done
He makes all the Pizzas with a great deal of feeling
Throws the dough in the air until it sticks
                                      to the ceiling
His minestrone is served straight from the pan
With lots and lots of Parmesan
He makes the best ice-cream Sundaes
His restaurant is open every day except Mondays

A Poem for Christmas

Father Christmas had some trouble with his back
When he bent down to fill his sack
Full of presents for one and all
He ended up in Hospital
On Christmas Eve he was allowed to go
He left his sack with a Ho! Ho! Ho!

Another Poem for Christmas

On Christmas morning it was a delight
To have Santa call during the night
As the snow was falling on the ground
He came down the chimney without a sound
And underneath the pelmet
Was a motorcycle helmet
And outside what was he like
He left me a motor bike

Cyril from the Wirral

A holiday camp was all I had
Every year when I was a lad
My mum took me there and it was her intention
For me to relieve all of my tension
I spent most of my time on the beach
Lighting fires out of arms reach
Roasting potatoes and drinking Pop
It was better than any 'Fish & Chip Shop'
My friend Cyril was really keen
To spot a Japanese submarine
Lurking on the shore late at night
He sent coded messages with a '*Pifco*' torchlight
He covered up his ears and waited for the boom
As a torpedo headed for the ballroom
He had this thing that it was kinda false
To prance around to a last waltz
For him it was strange fascination
To add to his imagination
It gave me the greatest of pleasure
Watching him dig for unwanted treasure
One day again he was acting the fool
He fell into the paddling pool
There was no way of holding him down
He said he could swim and wouldn't drown
After a week I was at my wits end
I needed to find a girlfriend
It was so sad he was all too much
We never did keep in touch

Under the Table in Malta

A night out in Valletta
Could not have been better
We were two young Lads having had a drink
Ended up inside a Clink

Acting like a couple of hooligans
Found ourselves lost inside St. Julian's
Scaling grand walls of a local hotel
It was the first step toward being locked up in a Cell

Reaching for the top was my mate's ultimate goal
Until he decided to climb a flag pole
The mast was bent over making it shorter
This being seen by the night porter
"You are making my night hell
Why didn't you ring the flipping bell?

Down into a hole waiting for the Bill
We were somewhere in Paceville
They arrived with gusto wearing night vision lenses
This soon brought us to our senses

The sergeant who was a bit of a dreamer
Insisted we both go to Sliema
It was somewhat of a strange fascination
Having never been inside a police station
After the fingerprints and a talk from the 'Screws'
We were then driven back to St. Andrews

If that not enough out on some bail
It was into the Guard Room and thrown into Jail
After some toast and a couple of teas
They then threw away the bloody keys

As dawn came we were both worse for wear
Unlike the night before we hadn't a care
The Provost Sergeant arrived, a much hated pest
Read us our rights under which house arrest

At ten minutes to ten it was another gander
Up in front of the Company Commander
With a quick march from inside the door
Stuart slipped onto the highly polished floor
With me a few steps back
The Major had a 'heart attack'
Clambering up the front of his table

He tried to make himself a little more stable
"Get em out! Get em out!' the Major hollered
Stuart turned around and I sort of followed
"Go back to bed and try to sleep it off!'
The Sergeant Major said with a cough
"We'll then try again and when you come back
Pull up your trousers you little maniac"
It was to be one of the biggest crimes in the last fifty years
It all ended in Laughter and Tears

Harry the Writer

Harry bought himself a pipe
And decided to become the Literary Type
In his kitchen amongst the utensils
He started to write with lots of pencils
On the stove whistling away
Was a kettle continually boiling all day
Wearing a 'Lookalike' Panama hat
A far cry away from a cricket bat
Put pen to paper with this and that
In his dark and dreary East End flat
He said I'm going to make a load of brass
But first I must find a shilling for the gas

Jimmy's Christmas

The Mantelpiece Clock strikes a twelve-o'clock Chime
Outside is the Watchman and cries everything is fine
Beneath the Gas Lamp his Lantern is swinging
Around Christmas tree we are all singing
"The First NOEL"
To the last sound of the last ding Dong bell
I say Merry Yule Tide to you all
While out in the cold the first snowflakes fall
There's a knock at the door
It's wee Jimmy Fry
Finding it hard to keep himself dry
With a tear in his eye and holding a box
Spare me a copper for Shoes and some Socks
Come in Jimmy Fry and wipe round your eyes
Before you tuck into a plate of Mince Pies
No wiping your feet here we're not posh
Just get yourself dry Boy then go for a wash
And in the morning a fine Christmas box
Of Sweets and a Shilling
Some shoes and some Socks

Joey Panzini and his Flying Pizza

The tables in the restaurant begin to shake
When Joey Panzini starts to bake
The perfect Pizza and Cheese Cake
He makes one hell of a din as he
Bashes the dough and puts it into a spin
Around the kitchen and up to the ceiling
He does this with lots of feeling
Joey uses more of the flour
To make it fly up even higher
It then comes down on to a base
After being in aerospace
The Pizza topping is made from various things
He goes over the top when he sings
In the restaurant he creates an extravaganza
When the candles are lit he sings 'Mario Lanza'

Christmas Morning

A little girl sat on a stool
We both played with her "Muffin the Mule"
A bag of Mince Pies to take home for Mum
It wasn't a Christmas, it wasn't much fun
It wasn't my Mum
Or my Dad's decision
To go on Christmas morning
To Shepherd's Street Mission

Cecilia Crêpe's 'TEX MEX' in a Can

"Now wash your hands if you can
We are all going Mexican
Here is a meal that comes in tins
It covers a multitude of sins
You can serve it up in a trice
On the top of boil-in-the-bag savoury rice
And if you prefer some chicken wings
Taco chips and other things
The Supermarket sells them ready to go
You can heat them up in ten minutes or so
Here are some I was sold
They have now all gone cold
Some are in a bit of a state
I think they may have gone past their sell-by date
We have now come to the end of the show
It's goodbye from Cecilia
In the Sombrero"

Bugs

We can see you through a thick pane of glass
In front is a window
We can see when you pass, Alas
You cannot see us in our dimension
In years to come it's your comprehension
We can move quickly into meetings and Courses
Fibre Optic away from your Human Resources
I wish I could speak I wish I could call
Maybe I am only a dot on a wall

MICHAEL ALTY

The Shower

Things went a little bit sour
When Stuart rigged up a make-shift shower
With canvas wall around tent poles
He used a tin full of holes
Suspended from a yard of rope
He was underneath with a bar of soap
I poured the water to lend a hand
As it cascaded on to the desert sand
The *RSM came and said, "What's this 'ere'?
This was Stuart's biggest fear
"Get it down you horrible little man
Before I put you inside your Watering Can"

*RSM – terminology used to describe a Regimental Gob with a Stick.

The Boots

The man that couldn't give two hoots
Stood by his bed with size thirteen inch boots
With brushes and polish to add to the lustre
He gave them a shine with a cotton-edged duster
The RSM came and inspected his feet
And said I can make you obsolete
He then continued to shout and ball
Stuart was only five feet two inches tall

Mr and Mrs Strange go to the USA

Albert Strange saw an Add
And said to Gertrude this ain't bad
Seven days travel including meals
This was the best of all the deals
A week in the USA what could they say
He booked the holiday right away
They arrived at Gatwick to check-in their flight
They were told the plane had departed the previous night
Gertrude was angry and shook her fist
When she learned they were not on the list
Arrangements were made to transport the pair
In business class for the same fare
The aircraft landed without calamity
After Gertrude mistook the flight deck for the Lavatory
At forty thousand feet
She sat upon the Pilot's seat
This was the Captain's worse fear
He said "Just get this woman out of here!
Never before in my hours of flying have I ever been so
                                                    scared of dying"
Albert and Gertrude left the plane no worse for wear
After ten-something hours in the air
The Stewardess breathed a sigh of relief
Until Albert slipped and lost his teeth
Down the gangway they went underneath
They were recovered and all was well
To start their holiday – they were known as
The tourists from hell

                                                      To be continued....

Mr and Mrs Strange in New York

Albert and Gertrude took in a Show
They found themselves sitting in the front row
During the interlude Gertrude said this is rude
She then got up and started to shout
They were then both shown the way out
On the side-walk they walked hand in hand
Until Albert tripped and fell over a hamburger stand
Gertrude pulled him up onto to his feet
As the mustard ran down the back of his seat
She tried in vain to clean up the mess
There was ketchup on the back of her dress
In the subway it was no joke
When Albert decided to have a quick smoke
He lit up his pipe on the train
Everyone thought he was insane
A policeman came over and pulled out his book
Gertrude gave him quite a look
Sitting beside Albert with a baseball cap on
They were on their way to South Manhattan
To the Police Department she would insist that
He was not a terrorist but
Just another naive British tourist
The Sergeant said after a few calls
"Why don't you both have a trip over 'Niagara Falls"

Mr and Mrs Strange fly back to Gatwick

A 'going away' party in the hotel
was laid on for the tourists from Hell
The fireworks began at eight o'clock
when the courier gave them a parting shock
An escort arrived in a Landrover
Their holiday was well and truly over
They flew back to Gatwick without a hitch
the aircraft did not have to ditch
In business class it was a treat
to see them handcuffed to the seat
A Customs man gave them a stare
when they said we have nothing to declare
Gertrude had only Maltese Lace
It was an open and shut case
Some weeks went by in the East End
A lovely holiday recommended by a friend

Stuart Again

The Sergeant Major said to Stuart
I hope you fly with a wing and a prayer
Because I'm about to fling you over the Square
"Here's a *Housewife' you little squirt
Sew some more buttons on your khaki shirt"

*British Army term for sewing and darning kit

Stuart's Revenge

It was a hundred degrees in the shade
When Stuart dug a hole with a pick-axe and spade
Temperatures began to soar as he constructed
                                      a refrigerator
In the desert sand where it was cool and moist
He lowered a bucket with a hoist
The hole was filled with lots of liquid
And on the top he placed a lid
Camouflaged with sand on the ground
He thought it would never be found
The Sergeant Major came, a merry old soul
His moustache disappearing down the hole
He said to Stuart, "Is this a joke?"
Stuart said, "Would you like to buy a tin of Coke?"
"Just you get out of 'er'
Stuart said, "How about an ice-cool can of beer Sir?"

Harry's Popcorn

Harry had a new idea
Whilst drinking a glass of his home-brew beer
This new venture was instantly born
When he thought of making savoury popcorn
He went to the market determined to crack it
read the instructions on the back of the packet
He said this should be easy to put into tubs
And sell 'Harry's Popcorn' around all of the Pubs
Harry started the process with a pan and some oil
And after a while it came up to the boil
There was corn on the ceiling and corn on the floor
The popcorn kept on popping and came up to the door
The end of the process was cleaning his flat
He said this is crazy I suppose that is that

Harry the Poet

In a Writers Circle Harry read some lines
from his latest book of rhymes

'On yonder hill there stood a cow
I turned around she's not there now'

That was good said a member
but what one should remember
One has to paint pictures in a
                 surrealistic light
Harry said I've had enough of this
Enlightenment bit Goodnight!

'Elgin Marbles'

Alexander was to grumble
When he saw his marbles begin to crumble
In The British Museum a long time away
From years and years of decay
'It is a about time we should all get
                              some peace
And send them all back home to Greece'

'Sushi Sue's'

There is a restaurant off Leicester Square
The food is good and prices fair
Behind the bar there is a griddle
They give you big plates with
Things in the middle
Crab is served with *Teriyaki* Sauce
Shark fin is brought as part of the course
Go to the restaurant it's worth a look
It gets very busy you may have to book
If you want to get away from
Theatre queues
Then pay a visit to Sushi Sue's

The Cinema

A movie was shown starring Ingrid Pitt
The audience said its Ertha Kitt
Down the aisles to the stage they went
Knocking down the Usherette
The ice cream slithered on to the floor
As couples flocked outside the door
"This here 'Flick' isn't much crack
We all want our money back"

Malcolm Ducket at University

The Principle rued the day
when Malcolm used the University
at the end of his term to cause a rumpus
and to blow up the entire campus
He made lots of explosive out of his own pocket
to propel yet another rocket
This time he packed loads of powder
to make the Launch sound even louder
The students thought he was a hero
when he reduced his office to a Ground Zero

Flash Harry

Things came out squeaky clean
When Harry fixed his washing machine
It developed a squeak and sprang a leak
That flowed on to the floor down below
He took it to pieces to find the fault
There was a big 'Bang' which gave him a jolt
Harry blew a fuse and a gasket
And found himself in the linen basket
In the back of the washer was a mangled sock
That was to give him quite a shock
He had to make a quick decision
To call in the Electrician

Harry's Fish and Chips

Harry picked up a few tips
To make the perfect Fish and Chips
For his friends he made loads and loads
He even invited 'Gary Rhodes'
To his flat he couldn't stop
And decided to buy himself a shop
People became fatter and fatter
All because of his Lager Batter
And after a year he too had to expand
To make the best meat pies in the Land

Harry's Christmas Trees

Harry was put into debt
When he sold Christmas trees on the internet
A truck arrived and there are no surprises
When he found them all to be of different sizes
There were trees on the pavement
Trees in the road
Trees in his garden
And then another load
Some ten feet high and very tall
Around the corner up against a wall
A policeman came in despair
'What do you think this is Trafalgar Square?
It was Harry's worse fear
When he said 'get these trees out of here'
The Council arrived to remove the mess
And put him into the local press
Harry said 'I've had enough of tree felling
I'm now going into Pyramid selling'

Harry's Crisps

Harry in France had another plan
To make some crisps in a pan
He filled a fryer full of oil
And waited until it came to the boil
He peeled a potato and then into slices
Because he couldn't thoil paying Parisian prices
The crisps were removed from off the gas ring
He said, they don't look right and are not the real thing
I suppose, he said, that's how it goes
When one has to shop in old 'Waitrose'

Pegasus Bridge

"It was on a bridge at midnight
Throwing snowballs at the moon
The 'Red Devils' dropped down from out the sky
Some to live and some to die
We think of those in 'Hoarsa' Glider
Paving their way as a path-finder
They shot at Mars from forty paces
They were the angels with dirty faces"

Cyril Rides Again

A year went by he's back again
Driving everyone insane
Cyril's back in the holiday trend
Trying to find another friend
With his plastic binoculars around his neck
Nobody cares and says, "What the eck"
He's on his own still out of reach
Lighting fires out on the beach
His mum doesn't care whatever the cost
She gives him two bob and tells him to get lost
In the maze of amusements he cannot understand
He finds more pleasure in a few grains of sand
Still trying to spot a periscope
Out in the sea he hadn't a hope
He was just a silly young dope
One day he fell into the holiday camp's 'Wishing Well'
Cyril thought it very funny when inside his jeans
He found loads of money
He lost his spectacles and in the end was pulled out
                                                        by a friend
They stayed together for the rest of the week
Back on the beach playing 'Hide and Seek'

Cyril Strikes Again

Cyril bought himself a 'Banger'
And flushed it down the loo
There was a loud explosion
And down the road he flew

Rock on Cyril

Cyril is back in the holiday mode
to begin another episode
and to spend a few hours
at a holiday camp called 'Middleton Towers'
In his drainpipe trousers and fluorescent socks
which came out from last year's Christmas box
He is back no longer a child
wearing a shirt like Marty Wilde
The kids thought he was off his trolley
In his specs he looked like Buddy Holly
Cyril practiced his singing in the chalet
He sounded a bit like Frankie Valley
And in the theatre there was a petition
when he won the talent competition
It was hit or miss the judges reckoned
when a little girl with a hoola-hoop came second
His mum in the audience wasn't his biggest fan
when he sang "My Old Man is a Dustman"
She stood up full of rage
Then he tripped and fell off the stage

Joey Panzini sings Figaro

"Figaro! Figaro! Figaro!
I am the 'Pizza Guy' fixing the pizza pie
Uno momento if you please
I'm using lots of peas
Powders anchovies and Prunes
Lots of tomatoes not forgetting the mushrooms'
I'm in a happy mood preparing the fasta food
There is nothing I don't know
When I'm bashing the dough
           Figaro, Figaro"

Boy Scouts

I was in the Scouts for just one day
This guy said are you ok?
And are you happy with your lot
I said I've just learned how to tie a granny knot
He said I'm about to go abroad
For my "Duke of Edinburgh Award"
I said are you going to the Himalaya
He said no I'm spending two weeks in Marbella
And how about an 'Outward Bound'
I said no thank you, and how does that sound?

Coal Hole

A spacecraft travelled inside a Black Hole
When it was hit by a lump of coal
It swirled around then into space
Landing in someone's fireplace

Cecilia Crêpe at Christmas

Now wash your hands before we bake
The almost perfect Christmas cake
First to show you something jolly
It is called a sprig of holly
You may not have seen this stuff before
One usually hangs it outside one's door
At Christmas another verification
To use it as a cake decoration
Do you like the Christmas tree
It was supplied especially by the BBC
Sorry about the lights
The wire became entangled around
                                        my tights
And as for the chocolate money
I don' think the BBC are all that funny
Use a bowl and a wooden spoon
And soon you will have the knack
The instructions are somewhere
                              in my paperback
Now here is a cake which is rather nice
Mixed together with sugar and spice
All is ready for storing away
To put on the table on Christmas day
Please do buy my book it comes with a tape
So its goodbye for now from Cecilia Crêpe

Cecilia Crêpe's Quick Snacks

"Now here is a snack you will never forget
All you need is a Baguette
Pineapple chunks straight from the can
Some grated cheese and a slice of ham
Now wash your hands before we commence
I know it makes a lot of sense
To have clean hands prior to cooking
You never know who is looking
Before you cut the Baguette into a top
                          and a bottom
Wash your hands if you have forgotten
Now poke your knife inside the bread
And if you prefer you can use your
little finger instead
Place the pineapple inside the dough
This will only take a minute or so
Cover with ham and top with cheese
You can put on as much as you please
Place under the grill until it starts to bubble
You can make this quick snack without
                          any trouble
And as part of the course
Serve it up with tomato sauce
Until next time I will be back
With another Cecilia Crêpe quick snack"

Cecilia Crêpe goes to Pot

For all you viewers who are into plastic
I will show you something quite fantastic
They come in tubs with a peel-off lid
An easy meal for less than a quid
In Harrods you will find them not too far
Away from tins of Caviar
They are new inside the store
And like you I haven't seen these before
You pour on water up to a line
Then wait a few moments and you are ready to dine
And as a matter of course
They have sachets of Tomato Sauce
Yesterday I was in a flummox
When people rang in with upset stomachs
Please do buy my book I don't wish to beg
It's all about things you can do with an egg

King Harold

"King Harold out riding on his horse
Came a cropper on a golf course
At a watering hole he was made to fall
When he was hit in the eye by a stray golf ball
Harold mounted his horse in a couple of ticks
The time on his watch read 10.66"

King Arthur's Fables

King Arthur phoned from MFI
This isn't a lie or historical Fable
The store said, would you like to buy
                      a second-hand Table?
Arthur said, is it round, and has it veneer?
I'll go an ask Queen Gwenivier
She came out from a garden Shed and said,
You ain't arf Arfa Daley
You may end up playing with your Ukulele

My Mate Harry

My mate Harry he had this dream
To buy a Russian submarine
To tow it into Tilbury Dock
And serve hot breakfasts around the clock
Hot cups of tea and sticky buns
They could go on deck and play with the guns
With rounds of toast eggs and bacon
You can even have your photograph taken
At the Captains Table he had this ploy
To give everyone a cuddly toy
On top of the Tower Harry would shout
"McDonalds eat your heart out"

Mr and Mrs Strange visit Malta

Albert and Gertrude discussed with some friends
A visit to the Maltese Islands
To go on holiday when it is really hot
They said it is a very attractive sun spot
Albert became very excited
When he learned they were into 'Manchester United'
Gertrude made up her mind
When they said they talk the same Lingo
And play lots and lots of Bingo
She said this is just the thing
They have even got a 'Burger King'
Fish & Chips and a McDonalds as well
Is Malta ready for the
      'Tourists from Hell'

They arrived in Malta without delay
To begin their holiday and a fortnight to stay
The airport Staff was to have a laugh
When Albert had some trouble with his scarf
They said he was entirely to blame
When it became caught up in the baggage claim
It was Gertrude's worse fear
To see Albert disappear
Through a door with all the suitcases
You should have seen people's faces
When the carousel came around again
They thought he was completely insane
As Gertrude pulled him off with her brolly
She sat him on a baggage trolley

With a torn shirt and a bruise on his head
She said you will soon be inside your bed
It wasn't long before the 'Tourists from Hell'
                were taken to their hotel

The Maltese Locals rued the day
When they both landed in St Pauls Bay
On the first day they caused a fuss
When they boarded a British Leyland Bus

Mr and Mrs Strange visit Malta continued....

Gertrude got up to ring the bell
She pulled the cord and down it fell
Upon the two
              'Tourists from Hell'

They thought of nothing better than
Causing trouble in Valletta
They called in the courier to complain

When the weather changed and it started to rain
He said, "Why don't you go on a trip to Gozo?
I can arrange a special trip soon,
Maybe to the Blue Lagoon"

Mr and Mrs. Strange go to Gozo

Albert and Gertrude decided to go
On a trip to the island of Gozo
On a ferry boat from Mellieha
It was to be the Maltese Coastguards worst fear
On board Albert bought two cups of tea
and then tripped and fell into the sea
Gertrude in a panic rang the bell
to save him from disappearing into the swell
The helicopter was scrambled right away
It moved into position without delay
Albert did not flinch when his pants
became caught in the winch
He went up and they came down
and ended up wearing a dressing gown
In St Luke's the doctor said you can now go
back to your hotel in Gozo

Mr. & Mrs. Strange go to France

Albert and Gertrude had the chance
to go on a day trip over to France
They saw an add in the local rag
and so Gertrude said go pack a bag
Things over there are cheaper by far
We can put them on top of the car
Makes sense said Albert off we go
It only takes seventy-two minutes or so
On board the boat it was very rough
Gertrude said I've had enough
Of all the crossings in the past
this is going to be our last
Albert went into supersonics
when he bought two Gin and Tonics
And after a sip he said there are
lots of peculiar people on board this ship
All this kissing and shaking hands is fine
but it is a total and utter waste of time
He said when we dock I want to turn
                              back the clock
Get on the phone and go back home

Madame Guillotine

The wife and I went to a stationery shop
And things came to an abrupt full stop
When we asked a madam for a Guillotine
She disappeared and was never seen
Again in the shop and after a while
The Manager appeared with a smile
It came to a head when he said
"Would you prefer a pair of scissors instead?"

'Rellies' in Wellies

"Little 'Bo-Peep' lost her sheep
And didn't know where to go
A farmer took her by the hand
She found them in New Zealand"

The Bundle

Zara and Charlie were in the station
when a woman was causing a big sensation
She wanted to talk to a 'Private Dick'
and goes by the name of Miss Wonderlick
Charlie said I've seen her before
Go downstairs and show her the door
At the desk there was a familiar smell
Could be the cocoa or Channel
Zara said she has already gone
With something she calls "The Maltese Falcon"

The Gardener

Dear Gardener's World
    Some of my daffodils failed to bloom
    The leaves are thin and twisting
    I looked to find these in my book
    But they're not in the Listing
    Can you help me before I go to pieces
    I think I have found a brand new species

Dear Wally
    We suggest you change your plan
    And put more holes in your 'watering can'

'Count Dracula'

In a 'Pinewood' Studio a tourist tripped
And fell inside a musty crypt
Covered in cobwebs and awful dust
To get out of this set was a must
In the middle an empty box
And on the end a clean pair of socks
In the corner a winding staircase
And looking round there was a face
This bloke in a cloak said let us be
He looked remarkably like Christopher Lee

Harry's Roast Chestnuts

Harry was back in the West End
following his usual Christmas trend
Roasting chestnuts on a stand
Around a corner off the Strand
As the flames from the oven went
                higher and higher
His white paper bags above caught fire
The smoke billowed out from the stall
And wafted down into Whitehall
In the street there was a commotion
Following on a loud explosion
Harry was acting rather coy
When a nut cracked a window in
                the 'Savoy'
The police arrived and put him on
                their list
As another urban terrorist

'Harry's Rock'

"Rock of Blackpool, it's no good
Wrapped in paper and made out of wood
One takes it home to break on one's teeth
God only knows what lay beneath
The letters show where it came from
Harry sells them by way of the prom
With rounded shape, they look like a candle
It is a surprise when they find a sewn-off broom handle"

Sung to the tune of "Rock of Ages"

Harry the Investigator

Harry having followed Inspector Morse
Tried a six-month Correspondence Course
He received his equipment in the mail
They said when you finish you cannot fail
With your Private Eye D
The magnifying glass will help you see
The small print underneath
That says it doesn't include new sets of teeth
He completed the course and was confident
To go out on his first assignment
Harry fell flat on his face
When he took on a matrimonial case
This guy told him not to pry
He ended up nursing a black eye

Rocket Scientist

Malcolm Ducket was dragged over the coals
When they found the cricket pitch full of holes
His rocket blasted off from the ground
He was trying to reach the speed of sound
The Headmaster was to have a field day
As one of his missiles went astray
The Air force thought he was insane
When he tried to blow up a plane
The kids thought it was a hoot
When his rockets came down by parachute

Harry the great Impresario

Harry thought of something clever
To take on Sir Andrew Lloyd Webber
He staged a play with a friend
To top the bill in the West End
At curtain call the queues had all gone
The Police arrived and told them to move on
He went home with an empty hat
It was back to the drawing board in his dreary flat

Poles Apart

An explorer arrived at a pole one day
And found his compass going around
                         the other way
He had a discussion with a friend
And said they had been dropped off
                         at the wrong end
He then made a quick decision
To end the entire expedition

The Avon Lady

There was a knock on the door
She said I've got something to sell
I said, I hope it isn't a flippin bell

Harry the Landlord

Harry tried his very best
When he put the Breweries to the test
He thought of a new idea
To sell Beef burgers with a pint of beer
On his first day he didn't do well
It was something to do with the fire bell
The sprinklers came on
The customers all gone
Leaving half empty pints of beer
That was the end of his Landlord career

Harry the Nurse

Harry is trying to pay off a loan
He works part time in a Nursing Home
He washes the dishes and cleans all the floors
When the Staff are all busy
He does all the chores
He serves tea and biscuits and brings birthday cakes
To little old ladies that he himself bakes
He entertains them and sees they're well fed
Then at seven he puts them all to bed

The Coach and Horses

"Bring me a Flagon of thy finest Ale Wench
For my thirst I must indeed quench
Bring me Tobacco and a Clay Pipe
Then bring me a Platter of thy Honeycomb Tripe
For to light of my Pipe
Bring me a Taper
Then bring me a copy of today's 'Pickwick Paper'
For the Mush in the corner some Cheese and a Flagon
Before we all board the next Stagecoach Wagon"

The Dewdrop

A dewdrop dripped from Cyril's nose
Where it came from, God only knows
Cold as an icicle, ever so brittle
Water ran down it, little by little
There was to be a sigh of relief
When it broke off and fell into
                    a handkerchief
Now squidgy and wet around the edges
It had dog-end stains, care of 'Benson & Hedges'
For his mum it became an exceptional issue
When he was forced to borrow a '*Kleenex*' tissue
She said you really must be quite insane
To go out naked in the rain
Late at night he rose from his bed
To have a smoke inside a bike shed
He said how did you know, mum, I get up from my bed?
She said, I didn't think it was a tyre-kicker from Birkenhead
At last his wet nose began to stop
To make way for another unwanted dewdrop

'Rudolf the Red Nose 'Dooin's'...

Santa is at Safeway outside his plastic dooin's...
This year he stepped out from a Bus
My Christmas is in ruins
I can't be doing with all this dooin's...
It doesn't seem the same
His ruddi dooin's comes with him every year
To bring us festive cheer

Inspector Coppini Caught in the Act

Charlie and Zara saved the day
When they went on stage to do a play
In the theatre they were sat in the audience
It became such a performance
When the two leading roles did not come on
It was a classic case of a has been and gone
Charlie thought of something clever
To get the act together
He bounced on stage with his favourite girl
She tip-toed across and did a quick twirl
They knew their lines
Because they had been there several times
At final curtain call
The actors were there in the box
They had forgotten to turn back the clocks
In Valletta it was such an occasion
When Charlie and Zara received a standing ovation

Inspector Coppini at Luqa

Charlie and Zara were assigned to a case
They used the Airport as their base
A man from Belgium was under suspicion
Then Charlie had to make a quick decision
To have the Airport completely surrounded
And all planes momentarily grounded
The army was called and put into place
While Charlie and Zara searched his case
He said to Zara I have my doubts
The bag was filled with Brussel Sprouts

Soap on a Rope

In the bath I wondered where is the toilet Soap?
I then looked up and saw it hanging from a rope
Not in a dish or in a tray or by the brush or loofah
But four feet high in the sky suspended from a doofa
I then reached up to grab the soap but much to
                                        my chagrin
A pipe came out the boiler and the ceiling all fell in
With plaster all around my head my toe stuck up the tap
It wasn't long before I saw a brick fall in my lap
Through the roof I gazed the stars, t'was more than
                                        I could cope
I then got out the bath and fell on that soap upon the rope

Robin Hood

"Robin Hood took off his boot
He had some trouble with his foot
Under an Oak Tree it was a disaster
When he tried to put on an '*Acorn*' plaster"

Sleepless Nights

The wife and I are having some trouble
With two single beds it's not quite a double
She says I am always difficult to find
When I disappear down a hole leaving her behind
I lay on the floor looking through a ravine
I then clamber up and then she says where have you been?
Pretending I am dead stretched out on the floor
I say go back to sleep you're becoming a bore
This bed is crazy it's a bit of a riddle
I drop off again and wake up down the middle

"Silent Nights"

Glancing at Shadows around four bedroom walls
The gas mantle is dimmed as night time falls
Down to the depths of the bed we would slide
An idyllic place where one can hide
Away from the dark and dismal atmosphere
That induced evil thoughts
And brought unwanted cheer
It was a place where we would be
In a dream world beyond reality
The snow was melting from white into grey
As a drunk passed our window to make it our day
When on Christmas Eve, the last knell of the bell
The drunk fell down a hole, and said bloody hell
It was back to bed with a blanket so thick
We had to lie down next to an Accrington brick
Wrapped in white linen to add to the heat
It was a pity it couldn't have been extended
                  to an outside toilet seat
Our parents came back sometime in the morning
when the cock crowed and the milk maids yawning
They sneaked into our room smelling of booze
to hang up our stockings while we were trying to snooze
And when we got up my sister would say
Not nuts, tangerines and fruit gums again mum
"Merry Christmas" Harold, and have a nice day!

Essential Commodity

You use it to wash your hands
It comes in different brands
In various shapes and unusual sizes
They are full of colourful surprises
You can use it everywhere even for repair
Cracks on the ceiling and on the floor
Or a difficult sliding door
It can be used to fill-in holes that appear on walls
To go along curtain tracks and poles
It comes in useful in the car
When a door becomes jammed and is ajar
Without this stuff there is no hope
Where would we be without a bar of Soap?

'It's Murder on the Nile'

"The tourists step on-board the boat
Each with a pocket book inside their coat
On deck chairs they all sit
Trying to find which one did it
The boats sail down; there is a lot to see
Some find more interest in looking at page three
As the sun sets it's a beautiful sight
To see them all go to bed
And turn off the light"

On your Bike

What was I like to buy a Bike?
On the fourth floor of a departmental store
A motor bike was kind of hard
To manoeuvre it into the goods yard
I was becoming completely miffed
When I became sandwiched in the lift
I had some trouble with the doors
They kept opening and closing on all floors
And what could I do one would say
I thought I was going to be there all day
If that not enough I managed the stairs
And people gave me quite a few glares
Pushing the bike in dismay
To end up in the Perfumery
Leaning down on to the throttle
I knocked down the occasional bottle
A floor walker came and started to shout
He then showed me the way out
I said, "You're a bit late, what are you like?"
He said, "There is the door, Get on your Bike"

Memory Lane

"Down Memory Lane there lives a Star
Where fish swim freely and not too far
From his lifetime dream
A perfect Yellow Submarine
He brought Barbara back one day
To share his favourite hide-away
Our memories will never fade
In his Octopuses Garden in the shade"

Stevenson's Rocket

A rocket driven by steam
Was Stevenson's ultimate dream
Abraham Lincoln was soon to scoff
He said, "This bloomin' thing will never take off"

The Garden Brolly

One day in the garden a gust of wind came
And blew our brolley on to a weather vane
It went round and round on the top of a steeple
Watched by lots and lots of people
The priest came out and with a frown
And called the Council to get the thing down
They stood and looked and had to think
It then flew off into someone's drink

The Clown

When the Circus came to town
We were entertained by a Clown
With a big red nose and wearing a frown
He was the star when the circus came to town
His tears were controlled but they could not stop
Falling on the ground of the 'Big Top'
The audience laughed when he fell about
Inside the sawdust ring
Every day he does the same old thing
To make people happy for a while
In his own make-believe style
And when the show has ended
For him there is always tomorrow
To continue with his sorrow

Russian Roulette

Inspector Coppini was called in to find
A Russian tourist who was left behind
The Politburo were to have a 'Beano'
When he was discovered inside a Casino
In Valletta away from the flow
He did not hear the ship's horn blow
Charlie Coppini stepped up the pace
When he found him in a Palace
Playing roulette always on the black
He was trying to win his money back
Charlie said cash in your chip
Before we take you back to your ship

The Man from Zanzibar

A Legend born in Zanzibar
Found his place alongside a guitar
Wearing trousers made of leather
He is going to live forever
An audience with the Queen
Was to be his greatest dream
His voice will be heard for years to come
He's gone back home into the sun

Roxy Music

In the eighties he was the saviour
Away from 'Punks' and bad behaviour
From Newcastle in to Scandinavia
Charmed the 'Yuppies' in Belgravia
He wears a Tuxedo is into Brylcreem
Within a strange voice he is every girl's dream
A likeable fellow with charming tones
He looks the part behind microphones
Now that the parties are over he hasn't gone
Still singing his song called "Avalon"

Ruby Murray

In my Club there is abroad
A name called Ruby Murray
Since singing songs she's made her name
With self-inflicted Curry
With Spices from around the world
Not far away from the faint-hearted
From Singapore to Bangalore
In Bradford it was started

In my Club there is abroad
A Chef and she's called Sue
And when you taste her Curry
Make sure it's *Nagra Vindaloo*
It is not the Murray that makes her Curry
It's all curried out by Sue
Don't strike a Match when Sue's about
It could be your *Tinderloo*!

The Eternal Eskimo

An Eskimo made a canoe
From Balsa wood and 'Super Glue'
And in his igloo late at night
Suffered from acute frost bite
A polar bear came and knocked down the door
And picked him up from off the floor
He carried him back, and in a trice
Placed him on a block of ice
It's not the place he used to know
Covered with frost and lots of snow
When icebergs melt and warm winds blow
He must be the last eternal Eskimo

Sky Diver

I jumped out of a plane one day
And bumped into a man coming up
                                 the other way
There were crowds and lots of onlookers
He said do you know anything about
                                 Gas Cookers?

The Car Boot Sale

When Billy saw the painting,
All grey with dust and grime
He knew it was a *Millais*,
And thought it was sublime.
His wife was not persuaded:
"It's junk", she said, "Put it on the back burner"
But Billy cried, "I'll buy it,
It now looks like a *Turner*!

MICHAEL ALTY

Man of the Week Award

They all lined up to perform a stunt
To win a prize and become the 'Shirt Front'
Of the week with a bow tie and jacket
Everyone there looked a packet
Looking smart all dressed in black
Each with a number one on his back
Jumped off the stage with a rose
They were greeted with loud applause
Racing down the ballroom to grab the wife
Someone said in the Audience
Why don't you get a life?
They had to race back to the Compere and say,
"All because the Lady loves Milk Tray"

Switch Off

"A loan piper marched to a highland drone
When from out of his sporran came a mobile phone
'What's this here?" Said the Sergeant Major
'It ain't quite like your silent pager
Switch it off you've heard the rumour
That one day soon you'll have a tumour
Put it away and adjust your hackle
Don't let it interfere with your wedding tackle"

Strawberry Fair

I once went to a 'Garden Fete'
And ate some strawberries on a plate
Not two or three or four or five
But six or seven and maybe eight
With Devon cream it was really thick
I ate a sausage on a stick
There were buttered scones with raspberry jam
Apple tarts and strawberry flan
I ate iced buns straight from the freezer
Then finished off with a 'Bacardi Breezer'
I thought I was on to a sticky wicket
When I was asked to play some cricket

Sting

My mate Jack was in repose
When a 'Bumble Bee' decided to fly up his nose
It bumbled about then gave him a sting
He shot through the roof and said,
"That bloomin thing has to buzz off, it is
                              quite stunning"
His nose will forever keep on running

The Charmer

The actor with the boyish grin
Was often seen in East Berlin
Spying over walls and barbed wire fences
Using *Zeiss* binoculars with extra strong lenses
In a film he caused a sensation
When he came up against the entire 'Zulu' Nation
Follow me Chaps" he would say
In the end they'd had enough and went away
The man with the blond hair and lots of chat
The Charmer who goes by the name of 'Harry Palmer'
There are not a lot of people who know that!

Going for a Stroll

This is the place where young ladies discover
The timely deliverance of a long-awaited lover
They stroll along paths towards heavenly bliss
In order to steal a much-needed kiss
Down a leafy glade where there is no one around
This is the place, they sit on the ground
They are not here to soak up the sun
But to have fun beneath a large currant bun

Lady of the Nile

On board the boat that sails back in time
A Dynasty Lady she is still looking fine
She reads 'The Papyrus' rolled back with care
Sitting on deck on a striped canvas chair
The boat drifts down
The 'Sun' disappears
She looks up and wipes away a few tears
With the same handkerchief she's used
        for over two thousand years

The Bells

Every Sunday at ten forty-five
Things start to come alive
The wife says, "What a Hinge and Bracket"
When bells start ringing and make a racket
They go on and on, taking their toll
We end up taking *Paracetamol*

The Butchers Dog

A butcher's dog went into a shop
And helped himself to a chop
The heist was carried out in such a way
He went back to the shop the following day

The Lion

A Lion escaped from Blackpool Zoo
And said today what shall I do?
Maybe a stroll along the Promenade
And then stop off to by a postcard
Maybe to 'Yates's' for a drink and some 'Coke'
Then take in a show for a laugh and a joke
He had a chat with a legless Buffoon
And said it was quiet for a Saturday afternoon

MICHAEL ALTY

Mansions at the bottom of the Sea

"Rolling along in the breeze I thought
There are ships out in the seas
Some are surged, some sub-merged
Some with masts and some with pasts
They all have sailors, let them be
In their mansions at the bottom of the sea"

The Land of Dreams

"America, the Land of Dreams
And the land of plenty
The land of opportunity
The land of big cars
And "I love Lucy"

The Man with the Golden Gun

With a silencer in his ear
Pulls the trigger without fear
In swimming pools he plays with the sharks
In Casinos he waits for the sparks
To fly off the end of his sight
Then he blows them away into the night
He uses power like a fox
And when his mission has finished
Puts his gun inside a box

Homes for Combs

In my life I must have lost at least a thousand Combs
Amongst the mounds of plastic
Some have found new homes
Down sides of chairs, inside drains and the backseat
                                        of a taxi
It is my guess that one or two behind the front room Baxi
I often wonder where they go it really turns my head
Last night my girlfriend found one beneath my single bed
They disappear without trace from here to God
                                        knows where?
They're not going where they should be going from my
                                        pocket to my hair
Inside the lining of my coat somewhere I'll have a spare
Just in case I lose the one that cannot do my hair
The problem now is all but gone my girlfriend is
                                        to blame
She called me up this morning and said, don't buy
                                        another one
She says she wants a break from combs and wants
                                        a heavy breather
With the magazine underneath your bed you're not
                                        much good at that either

The Kangaroo

A Kangaroo was aloof
When he poked his head out through a roof
'What is this?
And what is that?
I do believe it's my grandmother's hat'

The Ultimate Voyager

His position is high on a low frame
An admirable man no one is to blame
His thoughts are not of how he feels
He is more concerned with his own set of wheels
His electronic voice box brings it all back home
When we all have the occasional moan

He boldly shows where nobody goes
Heavens above somebody knows
He fades away with something in mind
To benefit the whole of mankind

He comes back to earth with something
                               much clearer
The Universe is forever nearer

Lights Out

A lone piper marched by the dark castle wall
When he fell over a large cannon ball
He fell to the ground there was such a big crack
To see all those bagpipes stuck down his back
They played a sad tune a final lament
To all pipers Scottish that walk the battlement

Mindless Adventure

"Ta nae maer gan oot, tis such a shame
The Y.M.C.A they are to blame
Nae maer crags and crevasse to ponder
Awa we gan oot, vast rolling hills to wander
In ta the lakes and in ta the Prairies
Some would say, tis awa we the Fairies"

The Monkey

A Monkey went to Longleat Park
And ate his lunch in the dark
He phoned his mate in British Guiana
With a look-alike plastic banana
It said, "I cannot take any more of this crap,
It's just another tourist trap"

Freddie the Olympic Goldfish

There is a Fish and his name is Freddie
He will only die when he thinks he is ready
He leaps out of the Bowl to play with the Cat
More often than not he lands on the Mat
The Cat picks him up
She's a really good Soul
She gives him a lick and puts him
Back in the Bowl
He swims around happily
His head has a Plaster
He only wishes he could go faster
He's ten years old now he's had a good swim
He nearly ended up inside a Japanese Tin

The Launderette

A Russian went to a Launderette
With so much money you have never seen
He put his trousers into a washing machine
They came out squeaky clean

Magnificent Men and Women in their Flying Machines

A pilot was to get it right
When he flew Transatlantic Flight
The Airlines were to bear the brunt
When they said he had to fly his plane
With only two up front

The Village Clock

Tick Tock, Tick Tock
That's the sound of the Village Clock
Tick Tock, Hickory Dock
Round and round goes the Village Clock
Tick Tock, here we go
There is more life on 'Death Row'
Tick Tock, it's a bundle of fun
Tock Tick, if you pardon the pun
Find the key that fits the Lock
The key that winds the Village Clock
Tick Tock, Hickory Dock
You can find more life on top of Ayers Rock
Tock Tick, and mind your head
As you climb into a 'Four Poster Bed'
Tick Tock, Hickory Dock
The undertaker arrives at Twelve o'clock
Tick Tock, Tick Tock
That's the sound of the Village Clock

The Ring

One day I dived into the sea
I lost a ring, where could it be
I searched and searched in the sand
It was gold and looked rather grand
The fish swam by without a care
One even gave me quite a stare
I had this feeling I had this hunch
It may end up in someone's lunch
My mind was bothered all through the day
It was out there somewhere in 'St Pauls Bay'

Moby Dick

Gregory Peck looking rather pale
Was jumped upon by a whale
You are sick
Calling me a 'Moby Dick'
The Whale said "Hey! You Ahab
You call for me a Cab
Because I'm just about to up tip your Gaff"
Peck limped back to Central Park
Where he was eaten by a Shark
'Greenpeace' said, "this is kinda groovy
And just in time for his next sick movie"

The Man with no Name

We know a man not all that well
What's his name we cannot tell
We think he is famous with a history
It is all a bit of a mystery
He wears a scarf and a deerstalker hat
He comes across as a real Aristocrat
The man is so silent we haven't a clue
We think he could be another Doctor Who?
We have often wondered who he could be
Maybe Lord Lucan or Lord Shaftesbury
He sits at the bar always the same
He is the man without a name

Lost and Found

On a mountain top we gazed at stars
No sign of life not even Mars
Out of sight from the world before
Not a glimmer or even a glow
from distant windows in the snow
The GPS came in very handy
when I bought it from a shop called 'Tandy'
The system worked but to our cost
found ourselves somewhat lost
The man in the store said it could not fail
As it was the last one in the Sale
On top of the mountain that cold night
We had some trouble with a satellite
Wishing that we were all in bed
We all froze and were rescued instead
The expedition went off the beaten track
And the following day I took the useless
                                              thing back
It caused one hell of a rumpus
When I said, 'what was wrong with a simple compass?'

Lady Luck

I was at the end of my tether
And wanted to get my act together
I went to a Casino to make a fast buck
And so I relied on a Lady called 'Luck'
At a table I sat next to a 'Betty Grable'
She said you seem to be in a bit of a mess
But don't you worry I am a millionairess

The Tadpole

"A tadpole went into a photo booth
Sat on stool feeling kind-a-cool
He pressed a button to change his Fizzog
And came out looking like a Frog"

The Tank in the Bank

One day a 'Crank' drove a tank into a bank
The staff thought it very funny
To hear that he didn't want any money
They gave him such a look
When he demanded a replacement cheque book
The manager stuffed the barrel with lots of loot
And then advised him to go and shoot

Albert and Gertrude in Valletta

Albert and Gertrude thought of nothing better
than to go on a bus ride to Valletta
The passengers crossed themselves before they fell
On the step they are the tourists from Hell
The driver who was into Tom Jones
found himself nursing broken bones
Gertrude gave him a one Lira coin
It landed somewhere around his groin
She said my name is Gertrude Strange
He said my name is Charlie get some change
Albert said we have only got a pound
The driver said how does go away sound
He was relieved in less than an hour
when an inspector poked his head from around a Tower
Where is your ticket can you explain?
I can easily put you back on a plane
In Republic Street Albert was the star
when he was thrown out of a bar
The Locals thought it very funny
when he said he had no money
Gertrude let out a rather loud scream
when she had some trouble with a cash machine
Gertrude the screamer took a boat to Sliema
On the boat Albert the dope
got caught up in the rope
He called the captain a bloomin old codger
and told him to fly up his 'Jolly Roger'

D.I.Y

My wife and I went to B & Q
I wanted to go to the Loo
She said you stay here forget about your bladder
We are about to buy a step ladder
And before you complain about your back
You have got to fix the curtain track
She said get a grip or I'll do it myself
We need some paint from off the shelf
I said what about a garden brolly
She said, just shut up and push the trolley

MICHAEL ALTY

Joey Panzini Sings Again

Si Senor der day go
Forti Lorries in a Row
Dems not Lorries
Dems are Trucks
See what's in em
Cows and Ducks

Sung to the tune of "Rock around the Clock"

Keep on "Rocking, Rolling, and a Riding"

April Fool's Day

Inspector Coppini went on the trail
to find the long lost Holy Grail
A scroll was found inside a jar
behind a wall in old Marfa
His investigation had to stop
when he found six of them
in a souvenier shop
He had to keep rather cool
when Zara called him an April Fool
You may laugh about the Chalice
The real one is hidden in Selmun Palace

Magical Mystery Tour

They played here
They played there
They played here there and everywhere
They played I've got to carry that load
down the long and winding road
They played something that no one can deny
They played music that will never never die

The Invisible Man

A Gentleman of standing and considerable wealth
Decided one day to turn himself into stealth
He fled away in disguise and despair
And like a burst bubble disappeared into thin air
Leaving behind him, a life in a mess
Nobody knows of his new real address
A face made from plastic with a Harley Street knife
A small price to pay from the 'Trouble and Strife'
He may ride a scooter or drive a red Bus
Away from the scandal and all of the fuss
It is more than likely he has a sun tan
He is the 'true' Invisible Man

INDEX

A LEGACY OF WORDS
(Alphabetical)

A City of a Thousand Baguettes	3
Action Man	43
After Shock	40
Albert and Gertrude in Valletta	166
Aliens	9
Alfred and his Cakes	28
Another Poem for Christmas	54
A Poem for Bedtime	18
A Poem for Breakfast Time	33
A Poem for Christmas	53
April Fool's Day	169
Aussie Bingo	10
A Wee in the Dee	32
Balls to Niagara Falls	44
Benghazi Nights	6
Big Night Out	39
Birds in Flight	29
Blindness	5
Boy Scouts	86
Bugs	63
Cecilia Crêpe	45
Cecilia Crêpe at Christmas	88
Cecilia Crêpe's Quick Snacks	89
Cecilia Crêpe goes Bombay	47
Cecilia Crêpe goes to Pot	90
Cecilia Crêpe's 'TEX MEX' in a Can	62
Christmas Morning	61
Coal Hole	87
Communications	16
'Count Dracula'	103
Cyril from the Wirral	55
Cyril Rides Again	82
Cyril Strikes Again	83
Davy Crocket	38
D.I.Y	167

Elgin Marbles	73
Essential Commodity	122
Flash Harry	77
Flowers of Anxiety	4
Freddie the Olympic Goldfish	155
Going for a Stroll	141
Halloween	8
Harry's Christmas Trees	79
Harry's Crisps	80
Harry's Fish and Chips	78
Harry's Popcorn	71
Harry's Roast Chestnuts	104
Harry's Rock	105
Harry the Investigator	106
Harry the great Impresario	108
Harry the Landlord	111
Harry the Nurse	112
Harry the Poet	72
Harry the Window Cleaner	48
Harry the Writer	58
Homes for Combs	149
Inspector Coppini	46
Inspector Coppini Caught in the Act	116
Inspector Coppini at Luqa	117
Introducing Mr and Mrs Strange	41
Italian Cuisine	52
It's "Murder on the Nile"	123
Jimmy's Christmas	59
Joey Panzini and his flying Pizza	60
Joey Panzini sings Figaro	85
Joey Panzini sings Again	168
Keep on Cooking with Cecilia Crêpe	51
King Arthur's Fables	92
King Harold	91
Lady Luck	163
Lady of the Nile	142
Lights Out	152
Lost and Found	162

Mabel Hibelthwaite	49
Madame Guillotine	99
Magical Mystery Tour	170
Magnificent Men and Women	157
Man of the Week Award	136
Mansions at the bottom of the Sea	146
Malcolm Ducket	50
Malcolm Ducket at University	76
Memory Lane	125
Mindless Adventure	153
Moby Dick	160
Mr and Mrs Strange fly back to Gatwick	68
Mr and Mrs Strange go to Gozo	97
Mr and Mrs Strange go to France	98
Mr and Mrs Strange go to the USA	66
Mr and Mrs Strange go to Town	42
Mr and Mrs Strange in New York	67
Mr and Mrs Strange visit Malta	94
Miss Lonely Heart	15
My Mate Harry	93
On your Bike	124
Our Cat	37
Pay up and shut up	35
Pegasus Bridge	81
Poles Apart	109
Pimroses	12
Pussycat	23
Rellies in Wellies	100
Robin Hood	119
Rock on Cyril	84
Rocket Scientist	107
Roxy Music	131
Ruby Murray	132
Rudolf the Red Nose 'Dooin's	115
Russian Roulette	129
Scooters	34
Silent Nights	121
Sky Diver	134
Sleepless Nights	120
Soap on a Rope	118
Stevenson's Rocket	126
Strawberry Fair	138

Sting	139
Stuart Again	69
Stuart's Revenge	70
'Sushi Sue's'	74
Switch Off	137
Symphony in Suet	17
The Avon Lady	110
The Bell Ringer	19
The Bells	143
The Boots	65
The Bundle	101
The Butcher at Christmas	31
The Butcher's Dog	144
The Car Boot Sale	135
The Charmer	140
The Cinema	75
The Clown	128
The Coach and Horses	113
The Dewdrop	114
The Eternal Eskimo	133
The Garden Brolley	127
The Gardener	102
The Grand Old Duke of York	20
The Invisible Man	171
The Kangaroo	150
The Land of Dreams	147
The Launderette	156
The Lion	145
The Man from Zanzibar	130
The Man with no Name	161
The Man with the Golden Balls	30
The Man with the Golden Gun	148
The Monkey	154
The Next Train to Waterloo	22
The Ring	159
"The Royal British Legion"	13
The Shower	64
The Tadpole	164
The Tank in the Bank	165
The Ultimate Voyager	151
The Village Clock	158
'The Whistler'	26
Titanic	27
To Hell and Back	36
Trinidad comes to Burnley	25

Under the Table in Malta 56

"Victory V's" 14

Wembley Stadium 24
Which is Witch? 7
William Tell 21
"WRVS" (Women's Royal Voluntary Service) 11

About the Author

MICHAEL ALTY was born in Southport, Lancashire, England in 1949. He was educated in Preston, Lancashire and is a former scholar of Deepdale School, he then moved on to study modern languages as a mature student at the Lancashire College in Chorley, Lancashire.

Michael joined the British Army in 1964 and served his Queen and Country in Malta, North Africa, Germany and Northern Ireland. He was for twenty-five years involved professionally in the Aircraft manufacturing industry at Warton, Preston.

He is now living with his wife in Burnley, Lancashire, writing novels and poetry full-time, hoping his books will appeal to people of all ages.

His enthusiasm for writing poetry and novels was promulgated during the winter of 1998 when he was standing on the platform of Kirkham railway station, waiting impatiently for a train to arrive to take him to a nearby town called Poulton, to undergo an annual 'Black Friday' ritual of meeting up with his fellow colleagues to engage in festive revelry and merriment.

Where Michael's first book of poems "Mirror Images" combined humour and pathos with a smattering of the cryptic, his sequel "Mirror Images Number Two" is of a more serious nature. To complete the trilogy, "A Legacy of Words" is an anthology, a mixture of modern contemporary poetry, reflecting his bizarre and interesting life. 'Harry' and 'Cyril' are back, also the intrepid 'Albert and Gertrude Strange'. There are some newcomers: 'Charlie Coppini, the man with the good looks', Joey Panzini, who doesn't exactly go by the books and 'Cecilia Crêpe' maddeningly irritating but quite endearing.

Other titles by Michael Alty:

The Guildford Boys – ISBN 978 1 84549 428 5

The Ghost of Latchford Hall – ISBN 978 1 84540 528 2

The Bells of Saint Clements – ISBN 978 1 84549 620 3

27 rue Mortain – ISBN 978 1 84549 686 9

Lancaster Grill – ISBN 978 1 84549 728 6

Purple Patches – ISBN 978 1 84549 743 9

Published by arima Publishing.

www.ingramcontent.com/pod-product-compliance
Lightning Source LLC
Chambersburg PA
CBHW060532100426
42743CB00009B/1500